A Cat's Day

Luke had a very busy day planned.

He ate his breakfast quickly.

He didn't want to be late.

His old cat, Lucy, was napping in the sun, as usual.

"What a lazy cat!" Luke thought. But he loved her anyway.

After breakfast, Luke got
ready to go to school.

4

"Don't forget to run my errands after school!" his mother called out.

"I won't forget, Mom!" Luke promised. "See you later!"

At school, Luke's teacher taught his class all about lions and tigers.

Luke could hardly believe that his Lucy was related to such fierce animals!

She was just too lazy!

After school, Luke
stopped by the
supermarket to pick up
some things for his mom.

The supermarket worker was very cross. Someone had made a mess in the pet food aisle. "I wonder who did it?" Luke thought.

Next Luke stopped by the pet store
to buy a new collar for Lucy.

"Maybe Lucy would like this ball," he thought.

"Nah, she's much too lazy for a toy like this!" he decided.

11

Around the corner from his home Luke saw his friend Sally in the clothing store.

"This store looks a bit messy today," Luke said to Sally. Sally agreed.

"Well, I've got to head home.
Have fun shopping!" said Luke.

13

"He'll never know about my busy day," Lucy thought.

She settled back down in her favorite sunny spot.

Lucy looked up at Luke and yawned. She was tired from her day. "He'll never know about my adventures," she thought happily.